FRAMED

Beautiful Simplicity

By
Gaylen K. Bunker

BusinessAllStars, Salt Lake City, Utah 84109

Table of Contents

Acknowledgements

I want to express appreciation for the generous contributions made by my wife, Diane, who has read and reread the manuscript many times and given extremely valuable input. I also want to thank her for helping me to realize the importance of accounting as a fundamental tool in everyone's tool bag.

Gaylen K. Bunker

Introduction

My wife is a very intelligent woman. Some time ago I encouraged her to take an accounting class. After a couple weeks she told me that the class made no sense. The terminology was very confusing, when they said "credit" it didn't mean what she was used to or expected. I told her that many of the words in accounting take on different meanings than what is commonly used in society. The words Debit and Credit simply mean left and right.

I told her that accounting is like learning a new language and a system. She must not try to relate what she was learning to the rest of the world. Instead, she must just accept the system for what it was, accept that some words have different meanings, and just go with it. Once she did that, she did very well and was successful.

Learning accounting and how financial statements are generated can be a difficult thing. But it is a critical skill that everyone, no matter what discipline they are in or where they come from, must sooner or later deal with.

Everyone works within an organization or a company where monetary values are important for the allocation of resources and the compensation of services. Therefore, we all should understand why money moves as it does. We all should have some basic understanding of accounting.

Gaylen K. Bunker

Saturday Morning

He put away his breakfast dishes and thought to himself of all the possibilities this beautiful Spring Saturday morning offered. He looked out the window above the sink at the thermometer hanging from a decorative post just outside. It read seventy-two degrees. His fingers began to itch at the possibilities waiting for him in the garden or perhaps that little woodworking project in the workshop in the backyard. It would probably be the garden; he needed to get those petunias in the ground.

He gazed up at the blue sky and then down toward the garden beneath him. As he panned across the scene, he suddenly caught sight of the new neighbor that had moved in next door. She was on her deck holding a watering can, lightly sprinkling a large flower pot. Wearing a skimpy white two piece sun suit she was enjoying the beautiful day, the exposure provided and the freedom to be outside. He thought to himself that if anyone should wear that kind of outfit it should certainly be her.

His thoughts began to drift back to the petunias when he realized she had noticed him at the window and was waving to him. A little embarrassed that he was caught watching her, he sheepishly waved back.

With her free hand she gestured for him to come outside. She stepped back, set the watering can down and motioned to the gate that separated the two yards and began to walk toward it.

"Well, I suppose I need to be neighborly," he thought to himself and worked his way toward the back door.

The two yards were separated by a six foot fence that generally provided excellent privacy. When the fence was originally built, the two neighbors, who owned the homes at that time, had decided to place a quaint white arbor that broke the fence near the rear of each home. A white picket gate with a downward rounded top complimented the arch of the arbor.

When he exited his home, he turned to see her standing at the gate. As he approached he couldn't help but notice how stunningly beautiful she looked framed by the arbor. He guessed that she was probably about thirty, but her flawless skin and excellent shape suggested that if she was indeed that old she could easily have passed for someone much younger.

"I'm your new neighbor Hannah. I moved in about a month ago, but this is the first chance I've had to make contact with you."

She was so physically intimidating that he could hardly stammer to get the words out. "It's good to meet you. I wasn't sure who moved in after the Razelburgers left."

"It's just me, but I'm in desperate need of your help."

Instantly, his thoughts jumped to plumbing or other kind of fixit job that a handyman might help with. He liked to putter, but never represented himself as someone with the knowledge to really do the job the way a professional might. "What is it you need?"

"Some of the other neighbors told me that you are a financial wizard, that you consult with companies and put on seminars teaching basic accounting and financial statements."

"I'm not sure wizard is the term I would use. I do consult on a whole host of business topics, but lately my accounting seminar has kept me pretty busy."

"I really hate to impose, but I'm in real trouble. My father passed away several months ago and left a part interest in a small company to me. I'm his only child and have spent most of my time doing modeling work and such. I know that physical beauty is a temporary gift so I have tried to get involved with the business and understand what is going on." She stopped and looked at him with all earnestness. "Do you have a minute we could talk?"

He turned around and motioned to a white round picnic table in the shade of a large maple tree in his backyard. "Why don't we sit down and you can tell me more." He led her to the table and took a seat, all the time thinking the contrast between them was stark. He was a rather plain nerdy type in his Saturday grubbies ready to dive into a work project in the yard and she looked like she just walked out of the pages of a fashion magazine.

She continued her story: "I began to think there were some strange things happening with the company. Things just didn't seem right. The heads of sales, production and accounting were all very nice to me, but seemed guarded. Then just last week I got a call to meet my father's partner, Victor Timothy in his office at ten o'clock at night. I thought it was rather odd, but went to the appointment anyway."

"When I got there I found Victor lying on the floor. He had been shot in the chest and barely alive. He motioned toward the bookcase and stammered: 'The shoebox, the shoebox.' Then he died in my arms. I looked around for the shoebox and saw a gun lying on the floor behind the door. I don't know what possessed me, maybe it was some stupid idea the police wouldn't see it there and so I went and picked it up. Just as I did the police came into the room. I've been accused of the murder and am only out on bail awaiting the arraignment."

"Someone set me up and framed me for this murder. I have a wonderful attorney, her name is Mary Payson, and she was able to get hold of the shoe box but neither the police or her see anything in it. It's just a bunch of financial records. Do you think you could look at them for me?"

"Well, probably so," he responded.

With that she was up and jogging toward the gate and her home. He was captured and all thoughts of the petunias flew out of his mind. He watched her all the way into her back door

4

and back again holding a small red shoebox. On top of the box she balanced a laptop computer.

"I thought we could use a computer to help, if that's okay?" she said as she approached the table.

"Oh, sure, that would be great." He took the shoebox, sat it on the table, opened it, and began looking through the papers as she set up her computer.

"I really appreciate you taking the time to do this. I have been in a panic since this whole thing started." Her flawless composure belied the turmoil she suggested raged inside of her.

"I think we're going to have to reconstruct some accounting detail to make some sense of all this," he said as he examined the papers. "Do you know much about spreadsheets?"

"Not really. I'm starting from ground zero," she confessed.

He leaned over close to her to see the screen and guided the arrow to the bottom left-hand corner of the screen where he clicked on the 'Start' button. A menu opened on the side. Finding a reference to a spreadsheet program, he clicked and waited for it to appear. "A spreadsheet is a grid of rows and columns where we can enter words, amounts, formulas, or references. It will help us organize the data."

"I think I've seen this before."

"That's great. I'm going to create a format to work from."

Desc.	Claims (Liabilities & Equity)					=	Assets						
Beg Bal	R/E	C/S	LTD	N/P	A/P		A/D	F/A	Sup.	Inv.	A/R	Cash	
													1
													2
													3
													4
													5
													6
													7
													8
													9
													10
													11
													12
													13
													14

When he finished entering the layout he turned to her. "I'm going to use some abbreviations for the economy of space. Let me define what I've created here."

6

"I have two groups of accounts. The group to the left are Assets and the group on the right I've labeled Claims. Do you know what I mean by those two categories?"

She thought for a moment. "Assets are things of value the company owns and uses to make the business operate."

"Excellent definition, do you know what Claims are?"

"Not really," she responded.

"Everything on the right side of the equal sign show who has a Claim on the Assets of the business. Even though the business is an entity separate from the owners or suppliers, the providers of financing have a Claim on the business until the obligation is settled. The equal sign is extremely important. It is the one thing that is absolute in accounting. The Assets must equal the Claims."

"Over five hundred years ago, in 1494 a fellow by the name of Luca Pacioli wrote a book where he described the accounting process. I don't think he invented it, but that is the first recorded explanation of how it worked. It is called the double entry system. This means that every time the business records a transaction, such as the payment of cash, they must make at least two entries into this grid, so that the Assets will always equal the Claims."

"When the Assets go up, the Claims must go up and when the Assets go down the Claims must go down by an equal amount.

Sometimes one Asset will go up and another Asset will go down."

"I think I understand," she noted.

Account for Anything

He thought to himself that only ten minutes ago he had no idea she even existed and now they were deep into an exchange of ideas. It seemed so natural to be with her, as if he had known her for a long time. He was sure it was her open and friendly manner.

"Let's list a few of the Assets that are pretty straight forward and easy to understand: Cash, Invn. or Inventory, Supp. or Supplies, and F/A or Fixed Assets. These are all tangible items."

"I've heard those terms, but how can you tell what the difference is between Inventory, Supplies, and Fixed Assets?"

"Let me see if I can make some sense of it. Inventories are those items that are sold to customers. Supplies are relatively low-cost tangible items consumed within the year. Fixed Assets are tangible items that are typically a high dollar value and will be used over many years."

"Think of the photo studio where you pose for a series of pictures. Many of the props, cameras, lights, and other equipment are Fixed Assets. What you are trying to generate are products to sell, the photos which are the Inventory. The incidental items, such as pins, tissues, and other disposable tangible things are Supplies. Does that help?"

"So things customers purchase, like the photos are the Inventory, incidental little things are the Supplies and expensive equipment are the Fixed Assets."

"You got it. There are two other accounts I've shown as Assets: A/R for Accounts Receivable and A/D for Accumulated Depreciation. When we talk about cash we can see the coins and paper money that represents an IOU from the federal government. Accounts Receivable is like a stack of paper IOUs from customers. They have value, and in fact can be sold to a bank or collection agency for money."

"Accumulated Depreciation is what we call a contra-Asset. This means it is a negative Asset. It shows how much of Fixed Assets or equipment have been consumed over the life of the Asset. If you purchase a camera for five thousand dollars you would record that in the Fixed Assets account. That camera may only last five years and then be worn out. Each year you use the camera you consume part of its value and so we record that consumption in the Accumulated Depreciation account. When we subtract the Accumulated Depreciation amount from the Fixed Asset amount we find what we call the Net Value of the Fixed Asset."

"I think I've got a handle on the Assets, but what about the Claims?" she asked.

"Let's take them one at a time. A/P or Accounts Payable are the result of the business purchasing Inventory and/or Supplies from vendors. If the vendors do not demand immediate payment and extend credit to the business, then an Account Payable is created. It is an Account Receivable on the vendor's books and they have a Claim on the Assets of the purchaser's Assets as long as their account goes unpaid."

"What kinds of Accounts Payable would a photo studio have?" she asked.

"I suppose the studio would purchase photo print paper and various Supplies from a vendor. If they didn't pay with cash then the vendor would send an invoice requesting payment after a certain period of time. During the time between the acquisition of the Supplies and the actual payment of the invoice the balance due would appear on the studio's books as an Account Payable."

"This next one is N/P. Is that another payable?" she asked.

"That's right. It stands for Notes Payable. Sometimes a business like a photo studio will run out of cash. Maybe their customers haven't paid for their purchases yet, but they need to pay their suppliers. Maybe they need to pay salaries to the photographers and models, but haven't sold the finished photos yet. So they go to the bank and agree to get a short-term loan to carry them over for a few months. They sign a note and show it on their books as a Note Payable to the bank."

"The next account is LTD or Long-term Debt. This is a Claim by people who have lent money to the business. Sometimes those people are banks, but they may also be individuals. Whenever the business takes out a loan, they agree to repay the amount at a specified period of time, plus interest for the use of the money."

"What is the difference between Notes Payable and Long-Term Debts?"

"Mostly, it is how long it will take to pay off the obligation. Notes Payable will usually be repaid within the next twelve months. Long-Term Debts will usually be carried on a company's books for several years."

"What are these last two: C/S and R/E?"

"C/S is for Common Stock and R/E is for Retained Earnings. When someone purchases an ownership position in a business they can be issued stock certificates that represent their share of the equity Claim. They give money to the business to use in return for a promise to receive all the Earnings of the business."

"So my father and Victor were owners of the business. I know I inherited a 50% ownership in the business."

"Your Claim on the business would be shown on the books under this heading along with the other Common Stock owners. If the owners decide not to take the Earnings out of the business each year, but instead leave them with the company to reinvest for growth, then we call this Retained Earnings. This account is like an Accounts Payable to the Owners and increases their Claim. So the combination of Common Stock and Retained Earnings shows the owner's total Claim on the Assets of the business."

"Are these all of the accounts? What I mean is, why did you list these particular ones and are there others that should be considered?"

"There are many other accounts we could enter into the grid, many on the Asset side and many on the Claims side. I've been looking at the year-end balance sheet that was in the shoebox and these are the accounts that were shown."

"Okay," she said.

Hunting for Clues

He entered numbers into the grid from a printed sheet he had taken from the shoebox.

	Assets						=	Claims (Liabilities & Equity)					Desc.
	Cash	A/R	Inv.	Sup.	F/A	A/D		A/P	N/P	LTD	C/S	R/E	
0	1000	500	200	100	6000	-1600		300	100	1500	4000	300	Beg Bal
1													
2													
3													
4													
5													
6													
7													
8													
9													
10													
11													
12													
13													
14													

"These are the amounts for the end of the prior period that we will enter into our grid on the first row as the beginning balances for this new period of transactions. The source is titled 'Balance Sheet for the year ending Apr 30'."

"I've seen that before. Victor, the man I'm accused of killing, showed it to me about the middle of May," she offered.

"There are several other loose papers in the box. I'm going to examine them one at a time and then try and make some entries to the grid for each transaction," he instructed.

"That's fine. I'll try and pay attention. I suppose we are looking for any type of clue that could help lead to who the real murderer is?"

"That's right. Here is a deposit slip that shows a $3,000 deposit in the bank. There is a note on the slip that states it is from the sale of stock. Were you aware of any additional stock issued during May?"

"No, that is a complete surprise to me."

"It could be a clue, but then again maybe not. We will enter it into the grid as an addition of $3,000 to cash and increase the owner's Claims in C/S or Common Stock."

"This is that double entry thing, right?"

"That is exactly what we are doing. The Assets went up by $3,000 in cash and the Claims increased by the same amount in equity."

	Assets						=	Claims (Liabilities & Equity)					
	Cash	A/R	Inv.	Sup.	F/A	A/D		A/P	N/P	LTD	C/S	R/E	Desc.
0	1000	500	200	100	6000	-1600		300	100	1500	4000	300	Beg Bal
1	3000										3000		
2													
3													
4													
5													
6													
7													
8													
9													
10													
11													
12													
13													
14													

"If you didn't give that money for stock then either Victor did or stock was sold to

16

someone other than you two. You had no knowledge of this transaction?" he queried.

"None whatsoever," she confessed.

"Let's continue, maybe there will be more. This next transaction is a purchase order for $4,000 of Inventory sent to Anderson Wholesale Distributors. There is a delivery slip for the same amount stapled to the back. You ordered Inventory for resale and received it."

"I see terms on the delivery notification of 2/10, net 30. That means that if you pay in ten days you can deduct 2% as a discount, but if not then you will pay the full amount in 30 days. So I assume you did not pay cash on delivery for the Inventory."

"I think that is our policy to pay some time later."

"I can't see anything unusual here. It seems like a pretty standard and routine type of transaction."

"I would agree," she offered.

"To record this in on the grid, I will add $4,000 to the Inv. or Inventory account and add the same amount, $4,000, to the "A/P" or Accounts Payable account for money we owe. With an entry on both sides of the equal sign we are still in balance, where the sum of all Assets is the same as the sum of all the Claims."

"I think I'm beginning to understand. In a way it is a system," she recognized.

"It is a self-checking system. At least we know we are still in balance; we are never sure that we put everything in the correct account though."

"So there is still room for error?"

"That's right."

#	Desc.	Assets						=	Claims (Liabilities & Equity)					
		Cash	A/R	Inv.	Sup.	F/A	A/D		A/P	N/P	LTD	C/S	R/E	
0	Beg Bal	1000	500	200	100	6000	-1600	=	300	100	1500	4000	300	
1		3000										3000		
2				4000					4000					
3														
4														
5														
6														
7														
8														
9														
10														
11														
12														
13														
14														

"This next slip of paper is interesting. It is a purchase order from a customer, Xtron, Inc. for $6,000 worth of products."

"Why do you say it is interesting?"

"Usually there are notations that are placed on the P/O when it is received. This has nothing. Let's go ahead and record this item on the grid. There is no evidence to suggest the customer paid in advance or along with the P/O, so I will record this as an increase in A/R or Accounts Receivable for $6,000 and a corresponding increase in a Claim. Do you have any idea which Claim would be affected?"

"Oh dear, since we are going to get money, I don't think it is a payable or debt, so it must be "C/S" or Common Stock. But in a way, that doesn't seem right."

"I'm going to record it as Revenue. When we sell products it is like we are getting a big bucket of Earnings that belong to the stock holders. So I will record it under the heading R/E or Retained Earnings."

"Really?" she questioned.

"That's right." He shuffled through the papers in the box. "Oh here is the rest of the story. It is a corresponding delivery record for $3,000 that shows the Inventory going to Xtron and there is a reference to the P/O number. I'm going to record this as a negative $3,000 going out of Inv. or Inventory and a negative $3,000 Cost of Goods Sold in "R/E" or Retained Earnings. So Retained Earnings shows Revenue from the sale and the Cost of Goods Sold going out of the business. The net effect is $3,000 of Earnings or Gross Profit in Retained Earnings."

| | Assets | | | | | | = | Claims (Liabilities & Equity) | | | | | |
	Cash	A/R	Inv.	Sup.	F/A	A/D		A/P	N/P	LTD	C/S	R/E	Desc.
0	1000	500	200	100	6000	-1600		300	100	1500	4000	300	Beg Bal
1	3000										3000		
2			4000					4000					
3		6000										6000	Revenue
4			-3000									-3000	C.O.G.S.
5													
6													
7													
8													
9													
10													
11													
12													
13													
14													

"What did you say Retained Earnings are?"

"They are a payable to the owners for Earnings that were generated but not yet paid. In this case we have Inventory that costs $3,000 that is subtracted from the Revenue of $6,000. So the Inventory cost the company $3,000 and then was marked up and sold to generate a $3,000 profit. All gross profits belong to the owners."

"Do you see anything strange that would give us a clue or shed some light on who really killed my co-owner?"

"Not exactly," He said as he rummaged through the box extracting another slip of paper. "Here is a canceled check for the purchase of equipment. It is for $2,000 to Jabberwocky Equipment and Leasing Company. Do you remember any new equipment being acquired by the company?"

"We installed a new computer in the accounting department."

"That would do it. Where do you think I should put this on the grid?"

"I don't think it is Inventory because we are not going to resell it. It is going to last for several years and so it probably should go into the "F/A" or fixed Asset account."

"Good," he encouraged.

"I don't see where it would go on the Claims side though."

"We paid cash and so it is a decrease in Cash of $2,000.

"Wait a minute, I thought you said we had to balance and these are both on the Asset side."

"One is an Asset addition and one is an Asset reduction and so we are still in balance."

| Desc. | Claims (Liabilities & Equity) | | | | | = | Assets | | | | | |
	R/E	C/S	LTD	N/P	A/P		A/D	F/A	Sup.	Inv.	A/R	Cash
Beg Bal	300	4000	1500	100	300	=	-1600	6000	100	200	500	1000	0
		3000										3000	1
					4000					4000			2
Revenue	6000										6000		3
C.O.G.S.	-3000									-3000			4
								2000				-2000	5
													6
													7
													8
													9
													10
													11
													12
													13
													14

22

"Interesting, so we don't always need to affect both sides of the equal sign," she mused.

He nodded as he pulled another paper from the shoebox: "This next document is a deposit in the bank for $5,500 received from Xtron. Evidently, they paid on some of the bills they owed. Where do you think we should enter this?"

"You keep asking me that. Is this turning into an accounting seminar with a quiz after each transaction?"

"I'm just trying to make sure you understand what we are doing," he responded.

"Okay, we got the cash and so I would add $5,500 to Cash and reduce "A/R" or Accounts Receivable, offsetting one Asset with another," she said with pride.

"Very good," He said pulling another slip from the box. "Here is a payroll note. It says that $2,000 was due for salaries and attached is a bank document recognizing the payment. Does this sound reasonable?"

"I think that's pretty routine, I would say it is okay," she responded.

"This is an operating cost or expense. It is a necessary part of doing business and shows value going out of the company. When value is lost then it is an expense."

"I know cash will be reduced because it was paid out, but I'm not sure where to record an expense."

"It further reduces the Earnings of the company and so it will be a reduction in the "R/E" or Retained Earnings."

"That's curious."

		Assets						=	Claims (Liabilities & Equity)					Desc.
		Cash	A/R	Inv.	Sup.	F/A	A/D		A/P	N/P	LTD	C/S	R/E	
0		1000	500	200	100	6000	-1600		300	100	1500	4000	300	Beg Bal
1		3000										3000		
2				4000					4000					
3			6000										6000	Revenue
4				-3000									-3000	C.O.G.S.
5		-2000				2000								
6		5500	-5500											
7		-2000											-2000	Opr. Exp.
8														
9														
10														
11														
12														
13														
14														

"Curious, in what way?" he asked.

"All these entries are raising a lot of questions in my mind, but I'm not sure I'm getting any better information about who is the murderer. Is there anything here that you are seeing that stands out?" she asked.

"Can we hold that question until we get to the end?"

"Certainly," she confirmed.

Pulling out another slip of paper he read, "Memo: $500 of depreciation on equipment for the period." He looked at her. "It looks like your equipment is slowly wearing out."

"I know we had to get a new computer because the old one was totally obsolete. I wouldn't have any idea where to put this…wait a minute, you said we record it in "A/D" or Accumulated Depreciation. So I guess it would be a negative $500 there."

"Score a victory for you," he said with pride.

She seemed to beam with the first big smile of the day. Her absolute radiance and natural beauty made him wonder how anyone could think to try and destroy such a masterpiece. Then he caught himself, could it be jealousy he wondered. "This is a reduction of value from the business and so it is an expense."

"You mean the other side of the entry is to "R/E" as we are further reducing Earnings?"

"You've got it," he congratulated.

She beamed again with great satisfaction. "You are either a great teacher or I'm a pretty quick student. I'll accept the former."

"I'll agree with the later."

	Assets						=	Claims (Liabilities & Equity)					Desc.
	Cash	A/R	Inv.	Sup.	F/A	A/D		A/P	N/P	LTD	C/S	R/E	
0	1000	500	200	100	6000	-1600		300	100	1500	4000	300	Beg Bal
1	3000										3000		
2			4000					4000					
3		6000										6000	Revenue
4			-3000									-3000	C.O.G.S.
5	-2000				2000								
6	5500	-5500											
7	-2000											-2000	Opr. Exp.
8						-500						-500	Dep. Exp.
9													
10													
11													
12													
13													
14													

"What's next?" she asked.

"There aren't too many documents left, I hope we find something in the rest of this stuff," he said as he rummaged around in the box. "Here is a cancelled check to Anderson Wholesale Distributors for $3,600. Here is another check to the IRS for the payment of income taxes of $200 and a third check for $50 to Pembroke Office Supplies."

"It looks to me like they are all a reduction of cash and so would be entered as negatives in the Cash account," she offered.

"Excellent, do you have any idea where the offsetting entries would be?" he asked.

"Not really."

"The first one $3,600 is a payment on the purchases we made for Inventory when we promised to pay later. It would reduce our obligation and so would be a negative in the "A/P" or Accounts Payable. The next one is an Expense for income taxes."

"An Expense, so it would further reduce our Earnings and be a negative to "R/E" or Retained Earnings," she jumped in.

"Good, the third is a payment for the acquisition of office Supplies and so would increase the "Sup." or Supplies Asset," he said.

"Do we ever reduce the Supplies account? It can't just keep growing because I know we are constantly using them, that is why we keep buying them," she wondered.

"We expense them through an estimation of how much we think has been used or we actually count what we have left in the storeroom, subtract that from the total in the account and expense what has been used up."

	Cash	A/R	Inv.	Sup.	F/A	A/D	=	A/P	N/P	LTD	C/S	R/E	Desc.
0	1000	500	200	100	6000	-1600		300	100	1500	4000	300	Beg Bal
1	3000										3000		
2			4000					4000					
3		6000										6000	Revenue
4			-3000									-3000	C.O.G.S.
5	-2000				2000								
6	5500	-5500											
7	-2000											-2000	Opr. Exp.
8						-500						-500	Dep. Exp.
9	-3600							-3600					
10	-200											-200	Inc. Tax
11	-50			50									
12													
13													
14													

"There is one last memo in the box," he said.

"What is it?" she wanted to know.

"It is the payment of dividends to stockholders for $70. I don't see a cancelled check so we may have to examine the bank statement."

"What does the memo say?"

"That's all, just payment of dividends to stockholders for $70. Did you receive a dividend?" he asked.

"I did. I received $20 on the 2,000 shares I inherited from my father."

"This is interesting. Let's record this in the grid and then summarize each column. That will give us an ending balance for the period."

"Is that all we can do?"

"No this is just the first step. We are going to generate financial statements and see what they tell us."

"Really!" she exclaimed.

"We are going to take this thing to the point where it will give us every bit of information we need. For some strange reason I believe in your innocence and would like to help all that I can."

"Would it be okay, if you don't mind, I'll run home and get a little refreshment for us," she offered.

"Great," he agreed.

She got up, turned and walked toward the gate. He watched her and wondered to himself how the morning had turned out very differently than he had planned.

#	Cash	A/R	Inv.	Sup.	F/A	A/D	=	A/P	N/P	LTD	C/S	R/E	Desc.
	Assets							Claims (Liabilities & Equity)					
0	1000	500	200	100	6000	-1600	=	300	100	1500	4000	300	Beg Bal.
1	3000						=				3000		
2			4000					4000					
3		6000										6000	Revenue
4			-3000									-3000	C.O.G.S.
5	-2000				2000								
6	5500	-5500											
7	-2000											-2000	Opr. Exp.
8						-500		-3600				-500	Dep. Exp.
9	-3600												
10	-200											-200	Inc. Tax
11	-50		50										
12	-70											-70	Dividend
13	1580	1000	1200	150	8000	-2100	=	700	100	1500	7000	530	End. Bal.
14													

His final grid with ending balances reflected all the transactions from the shoebox.

30

Recap What We Know

He looked up to see her approaching the gate holding a tray. A pale blue oxford cloth, button down collar shirt hung open in front revealing that she had slipped it over the top of her sun suit. On the tray were a pitcher, two glasses and a plate of pastries. He jumped up and hurried to the gate, opened and held it as she passed through. He followed her to the table where she placed the tray.

The sun had moved in the sky, but the table was still in full shade. He checked his watch and it was almost ten.

"Oh how foolish of me. I'm taking your whole morning and only thinking of myself and my problems. I didn't even ask if you had other plans," she sheepishly offered.

"I was only going to work in the garden, planting petunias. They can certainly wait."

"Sometimes I lose focus and have a tendency to only think of myself. Some say I'm self-centered and it is only natural because I'm a model. They assume I only think of how I look and what I want. That isn't true. For some reason people hold back and I sense a barrier. It really is a little difficult. I am conscious of my appearance; I have to because it is my job. I don't really think I'm any more self-absorbed than other people, but it is only natural for people to think that."

Her rambling caught him a little off-guard. He didn't quite know what to say and then blurted out, "I think everyone looks more inward than outward. I'm only too glad to help, because you are in a tough spot, I'm your new neighbor and I want us to be friends."

The last comment about being a friend seemed to really resonate with her. "Will you please be my friend?" she asked.

"There is no question about it," he assured.

With that comment she seemed to release some tension and relax a little more. He also realized that saying the word friend changed the way he looked at her. He sensed that every male is a potential predatory animal looking at every female as a possible conquest or challenge. He supposed that females see males in just the much the same way. He sensed the initial sexual tension between them, but now by saying the word, friend, it seemed to change the way they looked at each other. They were no longer sizing up and stalking each other, but together, as allies, were facing an external challenge.

"I don't know that I've had a lot of friends in my life," she offered. "What do you think it means to be a friend?"

"I've thought about this a great deal through the years and I think it means to sacrifice for the other person. Also, to ask questions with a sincere interest and listen to what they have to say, really trying to understand. Lastly, it means to encourage them toward their own success.

"Wow that is amazing. I've never heard it put so succinctly. That is really great. I'm going to try and do those things, beginning with you."

He smiled at her and then continued, "Why don't we recap what we know."

"I think we should. I know one thing for sure," she stated.

"What is that?"

"I know a lot more about accounting than I ever did before. I know Assets have to balance with Claims. I know Assets are the things of value that support Revenue generating activities. I know Claims show all the parties who have a financial interest in the Assets of the company," she responded.

"Not only that, but if the company were to ever go out of business and the Assets had to be liquidated or converted to cash, the money generated would be given to everyone who has a Claim."

"I also know that just as Cash is an IOU from the government, an Account Receivable is an IOU from a customer, has value and can be traded or sold to someone else. I know the difference between Inventory, Supplies, and equipment or Fixed Assets. I know that as equipment wears out we record the loss in value in the Accumulated Depreciation account."

"The result of subtracting Accumulated Depreciation from Fixed Assets is what is called the net Fixed Assets. That is what it is worth today as opposed to what we paid for it," he added.

"I know that an Account Payable on our books is the same thing as an Account Receivable on the books of those who sell us things and we haven't paid yet. They are IOUs from us to them."

She continued. "I know that a Note Payable is short-term obligation, like within one year, and Long-Term Debts are liabilities that span a much longer time, perhaps even several years."

"Liabilities, Claims, and Debts are all terms for financial obligations to those who have extended credit to us and have a Claim on our Assets until the commitment is paid," he pointed out.

"I know the owner's Claims on the Assets are represented in two accounts: Common Stock and Retained Earnings. The first is money they directly invested in the company and the second is a payable to them for Earnings that were reinvested in the company on their behalf and not yet paid."

She went on, "I also know that Revenues are the gross Earnings of the company and as value goes out of the business then we recognize cost and expenses that reduce those Earnings."

"I might warn you that I have made all this very simple with very few entries. If a company had thousands of transactions and entries, they would summarize all Revenues in an account and Expenses in various accounts. Then at the end of the period they would add up the Revenues, subtract all the Expenses and put the net difference into Retained Earnings. It is the responsibility of the owners to determine if they will leave all the Earnings in the company or pay some out in the form of dividends."

"So as an owner, I should be consulted as to if and when a dividend is paid?" she asked.

"That is exactly right. Not only that but you should be consulted about any new stock issued or any new owners added to the company," he instructed.

"I guess that brings us back to the issue of any clues regarding the murder. I was never involved in the sale of new stock or the payment of a dividend, but I should have been," she fumed.

"You're absolutely correct," he agreed.

She poured a tall glass from the pitcher. "I think whoever was involved in that is the one who set me up and framed me. It all makes sense now."

"I hope it is that simple, but we need to explore every possibility," he cautioned.

"What else could it be?"

"I'm not sure, but feel we need to go to the next step."

"What is that?"

"I'd like to construct some financial statements from the data," he explained.

Make a Statement

"I'm going to create four financial statement that will help us identify areas where there might be interesting things happening.

"Four financial statements?" she questioned.

"Yes we will construct a Balance Sheet, an Income Statement, a Statement of Retained Earnings, and a Statement of Cash Flows."

"What did you say the purpose of this exercise is?" she wanted to know.

"The grid we created is a way of organizing the raw data into accounts. We had just a few transactions, but if we had thousands we might break out more accounts, but we could still collect them into some organized groupings. Now we are going to put the summarized totals into a format so we can try and make more sense about what is actually happening. We want to do comparisons, see relationships and be able to make some decisions."

"You said there are going to be four different statements. Why so many," she wanted to know.

"They have different purposes. The Balance Sheet is a snap shot of the business on a particular day. It shows the position of the business, how the accounts are summarized into various groupings and if the Assets equal the Claims. It usually shows a beginning balance and an ending balance. It would be just like placing two photos of you side by side. One of them was taken last month and the other taken today."

"That is an interesting way to think about it," she noted.

"The other statements all show activity. The Income Statement reveals the results of operating the business and how the Earnings were generated. The Statement of Retained Earnings reconciles the change in that account. It shows the beginning balance, the increases to the account, the decreases to the account and how we got to the ending balance. The Statement of Cash Flows examines the change in the Cash account. What caused Cash to go up and what caused it to go down."

"It seems like Earnings and Cash are the two most important things," she interjected.

"All of the accounts are important, but they don't involve a collection of as many different types of activities as do Earnings and Cash." He paused and waited for her to ask another question, but she was quiet. "Let's start by removing the shading from the two columns for the description and the equal sign. Now I'm going to highlight with shading the Beginning Balance row and the Ending Balance Row to show that we are using these sets of numbers. We are going to transfer them to the Balance Sheet format."

"The Balance Sheet is structured to show liquidity. The accounts that are most liquid or nearest to being converted to cash are listed first and those that are least liquid listed last."

#	Assets						=	Claims (Liabilities & Equity)					Desc.
	Cash	A/R	Inv.	Sup.	F/A	A/D	=	A/P	N/P	LTD	C/S	R/E	
0	1000	500	200	100	6000	-1600	=	300	100	1500	4000	300	Beg Bal.
1	3000										3000		
2			4000					4000					
3		6000										6000	Revenue
4			-3000									-3000	C.O.G.S.
5	-2000				2000								
6	5500	-5500											
7	-2000											-2000	Opr. Exp.
8						-500						-500	Dep. Exp.
9	-3600							-3600					
10	-200						=					-200	Inc. Tax
11	-50			50									
12	-70											-70	Dividend
13	1580	1000	1200	150	8000	-2100	=	700	100	1500	7000	530	End. Bal.
14													

"We group the accounts that will be converted to cash in the next year first, summarize those and give them a title of 'Current.' Current Assets will generate positive cash in the next year, while Current Liabilities will require a payout of cash in the same time period.

Balance Sheet

Assets	End. Bal.	Beg. Bal.
Cash	1580	1000
Acct. Receivable	1000	500
Inventory	1200	200
Supplies	150	100
Current Assets	3930	1800
Fixed Assets	8000	6000
Accum. Depr.	-2100	-1600
Total Assets	9830	6200

Claims		
Acct. Payable	700	300
Notes Payable	100	100
Current Liabilities	800	400
Long-term Debt	1500	1500
Total Liabilities	2300	1900
Common Stock	7000	4000
Retained Earnings	530	300
Total Liab. & Equity	9830	6200

"I've highlighted the numbers that are coming from the grid with the subtotals and totals remaining without shading," he noted.

"Did you use every number from those two rows on the grid?" she asked.

"I need to use every one of them so that I will balance. If you compare the Total Assets for each column on the Balance Sheet to the Total Liabilities and Equity in the same column you should see the same number. If the numbers are the same that gives us great comfort that the system is working."

She leaned in close and examined the Balance Sheet that appeared on the screen. "I think I understand."

"I've also inserted a subtotal on the Claims side for the 'Total Liabilities.' This adds the Current Liabilities to the Long-Term Debt to give me a total for all those accounts where I have an obligation to repay where credit has been extended to me. I could also have added subtotals for a lot of other groups, such as Net Fixed Assets and Stockholder's Equity, but I wanted to keep the statement relatively simple."

She continued to examine the statement as he talked.

"You will also note that I put the beginning balances in the right hand column and the ending balances to their left and closest to the descriptions."

"So does this Balance Sheet shed any light on the identity of who is really responsible for murdering Victor?" she asked with some anxiety.

"I don't know yet. I'd like to finish preparing all the statements and then try to answer that question, if you could be patient just a little while longer."

"That is one thing I have never been very good at, patience," she confessed.

"Patience is the key to almost everything," he instructed.

"What do you mean?"

"I heard a quote once about patience that I really like---let me paraphrase it here. Patience with God is faith, patience with self is hope and patience with others is love."

"That is very interesting," she mused.

"So just hang in there a little bit. We will prepare the Income Statement next. I'm going to highlight almost all of the numbers in the R/E or Retained Earnings column: All except for the dividend number. I will take these numbers and copy them into a format that shows Revenue minus Cost of Goods Sold to get a number that I calculate for 'Gross Profit.' From that number I will subtract the expenses to arrive at the 'E.B.I.T.' or Earnings Before Interest and Taxes. We didn't have any interest expense, so I will subtract zero to generate 'E.B.T.' or Earnings Before Taxes. Then I'll subtract the Income Taxes to get Net Income. Net Income represents the Earnings for the period."

"It seems a little complicated. Why are there so many subtotals to get to the Earnings?"

"This is the formatting that I prefer. There are a lot of ways to structure the statement and in fact there are a lot of names that various companies apply to the statement. Not all businesses call it an Income Statement."

	Cash	A/R	Inv.	Sup.	F/A	A/D	=	A/P	N/P	LTD	C/S	R/E	Desc.
	Assets							**Claims (Liabilities & Equity)**					
0	1000	500	200	100	6000	-1600	=	300	100	1500	4000	300	Beg Bal.
1	3000										3000		
2			4000					4000					
3		6000										6000	Revenue
4			-3000									-3000	C.O.G.S.
5	-2000				2000								
6	5500	-5500											
7	-2000											-2000	Opr. Exp.
8						-500						-500	Dep. Exp.
9	-3600							-3600					
10	-200											-200	Inc. Tax
11	-50			50									
12	-70											-70	Dividend
13	1580	1000	1200	150	8000	-2100	=	700	100	1500	7000	530	End. Bal.
14													

"Some companies call it a Statement of Operations or an Operating Statement. It can be very confusing for many people."

"I agree. Why isn't everything standard so people could more easily understand?"

"I'm not sure I know why. I have a theory that complication is a form of protection for some people. The more confusion some people can generate the less other people can understand."

"Once again the numbers transferred from the grid are shaded, while the subtotal and totals are not.

Income Statement

Description	Amount
Revenue	6000
Cost of Goods Sold	-3000
Gross Profit	3000
Operating Expenses	-2000
Depreciation Expense	-500
E.B.I.T.	500
Interest Expense	0
E.B.T.	500
Income Taxes	-200
Net Income	300

"Why didn't you transfer over the dividend amount?" she asked.

"Dividends are a payment of Earnings to the owners and not an Expense of the business. Theoretically, it comes after we have completed operations and determined if there are any Earnings. Then the owners decide if they want to take a portion of those Earnings out of the business or leave them in. If they leave them, we call that reinvesting them back into the business. Once again let me remind you that all the Earnings of the business belong to the stockholders. It is their payment for sharing their financing capital with the company."

"You make it sound like the reason the company exists is to make money for the owners and not to provide a valuable service or product to society," she challenged.

"That's why we call it Capitalism."

"I'm not so sure I like that."

"I think you have just summarized one of the great economic debates of our time. I'm going to prepare the Statement of Retained Earnings. The only box I will shade is the amount I've transferred from our grid. The Net Income amount was transferred from the Income Statement."

Statement of Retained Earnings

Description	Amount
Beginning Balance	300
Add: Net Income	300
Deduct: Dividends	-70
Ending Balance	530

"If I compare the beginning and ending balances to the grid I can see that they agree."

Cash is King

"The last financial statement we are going to create is probably my favorite. In fact it is really two statements."

"What do you mean?"

"The regulatory group that first introduced the statement wanted everyone to use a format they called the 'Direct Method.' But most companies wanted to use another approach which they called the 'Indirect Method,' so we can prepare it using either approach. I'm first going to try the Direct Method and see what we get and, then do the other and see what it generates."

She looked at him with great curiosity. "I get the sense that you are really enjoying this."

"What's not to like? A beautiful friend I'm trying to help, a mystery to be solved, and clues everywhere we look!"

She gave him a sideways smile. "What do we do now?"

I'm going to use all the data in the first column of the grid, the Cash account. This statement will show the cash that came in and went out of the company. We will organize it in such a way that it will focus on three functional areas: Operating, Investing, and Financing. Operating will be those cash transactions that directly affected the Earnings process. Investing will be those where we added long-term Assets to the business, and Financing will be the result of the company receiving or paying principle and interest on debt or the receipt or disbursement of financing capital and the related dividends."

#		Assets						=	Claims (Liabilities & Equity)					
	Cash	A/R	Inv.	Sup.	F/A	A/D		A/P	N/P	LTD	C/S	R/E	Desc.
0	1000	500	200	100	6000	-1600	=	300	100	1500	4000	300	Beg Bal.
1	3000										3000		
2			4000				=	4000					
3		6000										6000	Revenue
4			-3000									-3000	C.O.G.S.
5	-2000				2000								
6	5500	-5500											
7	-2000											-2000	Opr. Exp.
8						-500						-500	Dep. Exp.
9	-3600							-3600					
10	-200						=					-200	Inc. Tax
11	-50			50									
12	-70											-70	Dividend
13	1580	1000	1200	150	8000	-2100	=	700	100	1500	7000	530	End. Bal.
14													

46

"I will highlight all the amounts in that column and show them as shaded amounts in the Statement."

Statement of Cash Flows (Direct)

Description	Amount
Cash Collections	5500
Inventory Purchases	-3600
Supplies Purchases	-50
Operating Expenses	-2000
Income Taxes Paid	-200
Operating Cash Flows	-350
Fixed Asset Spending	-2000
Investing Cash Flows	-2000
Dividends Paid	-70
Common Stock Issued	3000
Financing Cash Flows	2930
Change in Cash	580
Beginning Cash Balance	1000
Ending Cash Balance	1580

"The first section is a recasting of the Income Statement on a totally cash basis showing cash actually received and paid instead of what was earned or incurred."

"It's getting a little complicated," she said as she shook her head from side to side.

"You haven't seen anything yet." He quickly keyed the computer and the grid changed.

		Assets						Claims (Liabilities & Equity)					
	Cash	=	A/R	Invn.	Supp.	F/A	A/D	A/P	N/P	LTD	C/S	R/E	Desc.
1	1000	=	-500	-200	-100	-6000	1600	300	100	1500	4000	300	Beg Bal.
2	3000										3000		
3				-4000				4000					
4			-6000									6000	Revenue
5				3000								-3000	C.O.G.S.
6	-2000					-2000							
7	5500		5500										
8	-2000											-2000	Opr. Exp.
9							500					-500	Dep. Exp.
10	-3600							-3600					
11	-200											-200	Inc. Tax
12	-50				-50								
13	-70											-70	Dividend
14	1580	=	-1000	-1200	-150	-8000	2100	700	100	1500	7000	530	End. Bal.
15	580	=	-500	-1000	-50	-2000	500	400	0	0	3000	230	Change

"What I've just done is added row 15 for the difference between the beginning balances and the ending balances. Then I've subtracted all the Assets except for Cash from the both sides of the equation. This eliminated them from the Asset side and subtracted them from the Claims side. It virtually shifted the equal sign to the left.

Statement of Cash Flows (direct)

Description	Amount
Net Income	300
Depreciation Expense	500
Change in Accounts Receivable	-500
Change in Inventory	-1000
Change in Supplies	-50
Change in Accounts Payable	400
Operating Cash Flows	-350
Fixed Asset Spending	-2000
Investing Cash Flows	-2000
Dividends Paid	-70
Common Stock Issued	3000
Financing Cash Flows	2930
Change in Cash	580
Beginning Cash Balance	1000
Ending Cash Balance	1580

"Then I transferred all the change amounts from row 15 to the Statement of Cash

Flows for the Indirect Method. As you can see the Investing and Financing Cash Flows are the same for either the Direct or Indirect methods. What changed was the Operating Cash Flow detail while the subtotal stayed the same."

"In the Indirect Method we will show a reconciliation of the Net Income to the Operating Cash Flow. We start with Net Income, add back Depreciation Expense and then add or subtract all the changes to the Current Asset and Current Liability accounts."

"I don't understand. Why do you show the Change in Accounts Receivable as a negative when in fact the balance went up on the Balance Sheet?"

"When Accounts Receivable goes up, it means we did not collect the cash and so reflects negatively on the Cash account. In the same fashion, when Inventory goes up it also is tying up cash and so reduces our cash account."

"But when Accounts Payable goes up it represents positive cash flow, so how does that work?"

"By increasing Accounts Payable we are not paying out cash," he offered.

She thought about it for a moment and then said, "I think I get it."

"This is probably the best statement for offering us some clues. I have some questions for you," he posed.

"I'll answer them if I can."

"The company has a negative cash flow from operations, but reported a positive Net

Income. It looks like the problem is in the Accounts Receivable and Inventory areas."

She looked at the statement, "Particularly in the Inventory area."

"Can you think of any reason why the company would be building up Inventory?"

"Not really," she confessed.

"Also, with Accounts Receivable going up, do you have any reason to believe that some of the reported sales might be bogus?"

"What do you mean bogus?"

"Could you be reporting Revenue that is not real and simply fictitious to make the Earnings look good?"

"Wow, I don't know."

"From my perspective we have three areas to really focus on. First, we need to evaluate the large issuance of stock this period to some mystery person and the related payment of dividends. Second, we should look at the purchase of Inventory and see if that is an arm's length transaction. Third, we should see what the mark-up is and if the sales are legitimate."

"How do we do all that?"

"Is your company closed today?"

"There are several people who come in on Saturdays, if that is what you want to know."

"Hum, do you have access to the accounting office?"

"I have a master key to the building. What about tonight? We can go after dark, say about ten. I'll drive," she offered.

"That sounds good," he responded.

Surprise Visitor

After she left, he spent the rest of the day working hard in his yard. All the time, his mind was filled with thoughts of her, the murder, the clues, and seeing her again late that evening. He was filled with great anticipation, and yet he knew that the best cure for impatience was to do something else in the meantime.

Working so hard in the yard all day long had made him physically tired by the time evening came. He looked at his watch and it was eight-thirty. Putting his tools away in the shed, he went into the house and up to his room on the second floor. He removed his work clothes, showered, and had just pulled his pants on when he heard the back door open and close.

He froze and remembered that when he came in he hadn't locked the door. Listening very quietly, he heard someone come up the back stairs to the kitchen. Then he heard noises from the kitchen and he moved to the landing overlooking the hallway that led to the kitchen door.

Suddenly, the light in the kitchen went on and Hannah came walking through the door. She was carrying a basket of bread, stopped, looked up at him and said, "Where do you want to eat? Oh, I hope you don't mind. I've noticed you working so hard all day long and decided to sacrifice for a friend. I've made dinner."

He pointed through another door. "In there is the dining room, but why don't we just eat in the kitchen, if that is okay. I'll finish dressing." He turned and retreated back into his room.

As they were finishing dinner he asked, "That was excellent so now tell me a little more about what the company does and who you suspect."

"We sell retail pet Supplies, but we mostly contract with large corporate accounts like zoos and such. The three people I suspect most would be Woodrow Peck, head of sales, Margaret Pie, head of accounting, and Humperdinck Bird, head of production. Any of them could be involved in the issuance of new stock. Peck or Pie I suspect could be behind the increase in Accounts Receivable and Bird may have something to do with the build-up in Inventory. Then again, it could be any of them," she concluded.

He looked out the window and then at his watch. "It's dark now, why don't we head for the office."

When they arrived at the office the blackness of the night engulfed them. She parked down the street and they walked to the building. As she was unlocking the back door, she paused. "Did you hear that?"

He listed, "I don't hear anything."

"I heard something," she said as she paused a bit longer and then pushed the door open and they entered. She pulled a small flashlight from her purse and clicked it on. "What are we looking for?"

"We need to get to the accounting records."

"This way," she said and led them forward. They came to the locked door of an office in a far corner. "I don't know if my key will get us in here. Wow, it does," she said with some surprise. She moved to one corner as he hurried quickly to the desk and began searching the drawers. He turned on the computer and as he waited for it to boot up he searched for keys that would unlock various filing cabinets that lined one wall.

He noticed a small area rug in front of the desk and one corner appeared to be rumpled. He lifted it and found two keys. He handed them to Hannah, "You go through those drawers and look for copies of invoices and purchase orders," he instructed.

Back at the computer he searched the icons for files and folders on the screen. "I'm not sure if I can get anything out of this, and we will need passwords to get into anything that will really do us any good."

"I don't know if this will help," she said standing in front of an open file drawer and holding a folder open. She handed it over and he examined it.

"These are copies of your invoices billing for products that have been shipped. It looks like you are charging $75 per 100 pounds of exotic bird seed. Do you see anywhere there a folder for purchase orders?" he said as the light of the computer screen illuminated his face and the documents he was examining.

She directed the flashlight across the various folders. "Here it is." She handed the folder to him.

He scanned the pages in the folder. "It appears that you are paying $50 for the same 100 pounds of exotic bird seed."

"What does that mean?" she asked.

"On first blush, it looks like you are adding a 50% mark-up on products sold, at least on this item." He quickly reviewed other pages from both folders. "It looks like that is pretty consistent."

"I still don't get it," she confessed.

"The entry we made into the grid for Revenue was $6,000 and the related delivery of Inventory was for $3,000. That is a one hundred percent mark-up, not a fifty percent."

"So, what does that mean?"

"I think someone may be padding the Revenue to make the financial statements look good."

"Oh, that is terrible. We may be in deep financial trouble and not know it."

"That's right. In addition to that you have a large build-up of Inventory that is potentially not going to be sold. That would mean more losses for the company. Look and see if you can find a file with stockholder information."

After examining all the folders in that drawer, she closed it and began going through other drawers. He continued to struggle with the computer, trying to access information that could help.

"I think I've got it, look here!" she exclaimed. She handed him a folder and he read the tab that said 'stock certificates.'

"I didn't know anyone still issued certificates," he said as he opened the file. "Well, there are no real certificates in here, but there is a listing of what stock was issued, the date and to whom. That last certificate for 3,000 shares went to..." he stopped reading abruptly as the sound of a wastebasket being kicked over echoed from the offices outside where they were.

"Someone is out there," she whispered as she clicked off her flashlight.

He put his forefinger to his lips to signal for her to be quiet.

Reconciliation

They froze, silently listening and then heard the sound of someone entering the office next to where they were.

The two individuals in the accounting office slowly moved to the door they had come in through. Hannah slowly opened the door and peered out into the large open area where several desks were clustered in the middle. They eased their way out of the office and as they did noticed the door to the next office was closed, but the light of a flashlight danced on the floor beneath it.

They moved to the cluster of desks and then heard a door begin to open. They crouched down behind one of the desks as a man came out of the office, turned and went to the accounting office. He pushed the door open, stepped in, and looked around quickly searching for the reason the computer screen was on. Then he wheeled and scanned the open area.

Hannah jumped up and began to run for the front door. Her friend immediately followed her. Taken aback by the sudden burst, the intruder was caught by surprise. He hesitated only a few seconds, but was soon giving chase.

The front door jammed. Hannah turned and was off leading the trio down a long hallway. At the end she bolted to the left and up a flight of stairs to a landing and through a door onto the roof.

The roof was a large flat area with trellises, birdhouses and statuary for the demonstration of bird related products. Hannah dodged in and out of the maze toward a far ledge where an iron fire escape led over and down to the ground.

As Hannah and her friend approached the escape, the man following them had closed the distance and cut them off. He jumped in front of them and they froze. He was holding a gun.

"So it is you, Woodrow. You are the one who killed Victor and have tried to frame me. You are the one who has been padding the Revenue to make the company look better than it really is."

"That's right, and you are the one who coerced the company to issue stock to you so you could take the company over once the two principals were out of the way," her friend added.

"I'm sorry to hear that you have figured it all out. You probably know that I have a life insurance policy on the owners that will set me up with millions. Now if you two love birds will accommodate me and commit suicide by jumping to your deaths, everything will be fine."

Just then Hannah's accomplice raised his right arm above the head of the gunman and began to draw it across from left to right and as he did said, "Balance Sheet." Then he lowered it a bit and drawing it across from left to right again said, "Balance Sheet."

The gunman looked on in confusion as though he were watching an Indian medicine man inscribe an oath to some god. "What are you doing?" he cursed.

The friend then placed his hand high to the right and lowering it said, "Income Statement." Then to the left in a parallel fashion lowered it saying, "Statement of Cash Flows."

As he dropped his hand with the gunman's eyes glued to the motion, Hannah swung the bag she was carrying as hard as she could and caught the gunman squarely on the side of the head. He fell like a load of bricks and was unconscious with the gun lying beside him.

"That flashlight must be heavy," she offered.

"We know he's the murderer and he knows he's the murderer, but how do we convince the authorities of the truth? We have a paper trail that supports motive, but it still might be a challenge."

"I don't think so," Hannah announced as she produced a cell phone. "I have recorded everything."

"How beautifully simple," was all he could say.

Summary of Concepts

2/10, net 30: If you pay in ten days you can deduct 2% as a discount, but if not then you will pay the full amount in 30 days. Page 16

Accounts Payable: Accounts Payable are the result of the business purchasing Inventory and/or Supplies from vendors, who have a Claim on the Assets of the business as long as their account goes unpaid. Page 9-10

Accounts Receivable: Accounts Receivable are like a stack of IOUs from customers. They have value, and in fact can be sold to a bank or collection agency for money. Page 9

Accumulated Depreciation: Accumulated Depreciation is what we call a contra-Asset. It shows how much of Fixed Assets or equipment have been consumed over the life of the Asset. When we subtract the Accumulated Depreciation amount from the Fixed Asset amount we find what we call the Net Value of the Fixed Assets. Page 9

Assets and Claims: I have two groups of accounts. The group in the left are Assets and the group on the right I've labeled Claims. Page 7

Assets: Assets are things of value the company owns and uses to make the business operate. Page 7

Balance Sheet: The Balance Sheet is a snapshot of the business on a particular day. It shows the position of the business, how the accounts are summarized into various groupings and if the Assets equal the Claims. Page 35

Balance: The equal sign is extremely important. It is the one thing that is absolute in accounting. The Assets must equal the Claims. Page 7

Capitalism: The reason the company exists is to make money for the owners and not to provide a valuable service or product to society. That's why we call it capitalism. Page 43

Claims: Everything on the right side of the equal sign shows who has a Claim on the Assets of the business. Page 7

Common Stock: When someone purchases an ownership position in a business they can be issued stock certificates that represent their share of the equity Claim. They give money to the business to use in return for a promise to receive all the Earnings of the business. Page 11

Cost of Goods Sold: When Inventory is delivered to the customer, an Asset is reduced and goes out of the business. This reduces the Earnings of the business and is recorded as Cost of Goods Sold in the Retained Earnings account. Page 18

Current Accounts: Current Assets will generate positive cash in the next year, while Current Liabilities will require a payout of cash in the same time period. Page 38

Dividends: Dividends are a payment of Earnings to the owners and not an expense of the business. Page 42

Double Entry System: The double entry system means that every time the business records a transaction they must make at least two entries. Assets must always equal the Claims. Page 7

E.B.I.T.: The Earnings Before Interest and Taxes is the Gross Profit minus all the operating expenses. Page 40

E.B.T.: Earnings Before Taxes is the E.B.I.T. less any interest expense. Page 40

Equality: If you compare the Total Assets for each column on the Balance Sheet to the Total Liabilities and Equity in the same column, you should see the same number. Page 39

Financing Activity: Financing activity is the result of the company receiving or paying principle and interest on debt in addition to receiving or distributing money to and from the stockholders and any related dividends.

Gross Profit: Revenue minus Cost of Goods Sold is the Gross Profit. Page 40

Impatience: The best cure for impatience is to do something else in the meantime. Page 51

Income Statement: The Income Statement reveals the results of operating the business and how the Earnings were generated. Page 36

Investing Activity: Investing activity is the result of purchasing or selling Long-Term Assets for the business.

Liquidation: If the company was to go out of business and the Assets had to be liquidated or converted to cash, the money generated would be given to everyone who has a Claim. Page 32

Liquidity: The Balance Sheet is structured to show liquidity. The accounts that are most liquid or nearest to being converted to cash are listed first and those that are furthest away listed last. Page 36-37

Long-Term Debts: This is a Claim by people or banks who have lent money to the business.

The company agrees to repay the amount at a specified period of time, plus interest for the use of the money. It is usually for several years. Page 10-11

Net Income: Subtract Income Taxes from E.B.T. to get Net Income. Net Income represents the Earnings for the period. Page 41

Notes Payable: Companies go to a bank and agree to get a short-term loan to carry them over for a few months. They sign a note and show it on their books as a Note Payable to the bank. Page 10

Operating Cash Flows (Direct Method): The first section of the Statement of Cash Flows is a recasting of the Income Statement on a totally cash basis. Page 46

Operating Cash Flows (Indirect Method): This will show a reconciliation of the Net Income to the Operating Cash Flow. We start with Net Income, add back Depreciation Expense and then add or subtract all the changes to the Current Asset and Current Liability accounts. Page 49
Page 5

Patience: Patience with God is faith, patience with self is hope and patience with others is love. Page 40

Retained Earnings: Earnings that are left in the business for growth instead of paid out to the owners is Retained Earnings. This is like an Accounts Payable to the owners and increases their Claim. Page 11

Revenue: When we sell products it is like we are getting a big bucket of Earnings that belong to the stock holders. We record this in Retained Earnings. Page 18

Spreadsheets: A spreadsheet is a grid of rows and columns where we can enter words, amounts, formulas, or references. It will help us organize the data.

Statement of Cash Flows: The Statement of Cash Flows examines the change in the cash account, what caused cash to go up and what caused it to go down. Page 36

Statement of Retained Earnings: The Statement of Retained Earnings reconciles the change in that account. It shows the beginning balance, the increases to the account, the decreases to the account and how we got to the ending balance. Page 36

Tangible Assets: Cash, Inventory, Supplies, and Fixed Assets are all tangible Assets. Page 8

Total Liabilities: This is the sum of Current Liabilities and Long-Term Debt. Page 39